Super Strawberries

By Heather Hammonds

Strawberries to Eat

Do you like strawberries?

Strawberries are sweet and red.

They are very good for you.

You can eat strawberries.

You can eat strawberries
with ice cream.

You can eat strawberry jam, too.

Strawberry Plants

Strawberries are fruit.
The fruit grows
on strawberry plants.

Strawberry plants are small plants.
They have lots of green leaves.

Flowers grow on strawberry plants.
The flowers turn
into little green strawberries.

The little green strawberries
grow big and sweet and red.

flowers

leaves

fruit

roots

A strawberry plant

Strawberry Seeds

Look at this strawberry.

It has lots of little seeds.

The seeds are on the outside
of the strawberry.

Some strawberry plants
grow from seeds.

You can put the strawberry seeds in the ground.
The seeds will grow into new strawberry plants.
Sweet, red strawberries will grow on the plants.

Strawberry Runners

Look at this big strawberry plant.

Can you see the new plants?

The new plants are called runners.

Most strawberry plants
grow new plants.

runners

Big strawberry plants
have lots of runners.
The runners grow
into big plants, too.
The strawberry plants
grow and grow!

Strawberry Farms

Some strawberry plants grow
on strawberry farms.
The strawberries grow in long rows.

Some farmers put plastic
on the ground first.
They cut holes in the plastic.

The strawberry plants
go down into the soil.
Then they grow out of the holes
in the plastic.

The strawberries grow
on top of the plastic.
The plastic keeps the grass
and weeds away.

Growing Strawberries

Strawberry plants
need lots of water
and plant food.
They need lots of sun, too.
Flowers grow
on the strawberry plants
when it is warm and sunny.

The flowers turn
into little green strawberries.
The little green strawberries
grow big and sweet and red.

Soon it is time to pick
the strawberries!

Strawberries at Home

You can grow strawberry plants at home.

Put the strawberry plants in the ground, or put them in a pot like this.

Give your strawberry plants
lots of water.
Give them lots of plant food, too.
Your strawberry plants
will get bigger.
You can watch flowers grow
on the plants.

Then you will have lots of sweet, red strawberries to eat!